Saint
ELIZABETH ANN SETON

W9-BAF-445

By REV. LAWRENCE G. LOVASIK, S.V.D.
Divine Word Missionary

NIHIL OBSTAT: Daniel V. Flynn, J.C.D., *Censor Librorum*
IMPRIMATUR: ✠ Joseph T. O'Keefe, D.D., *Vicar General, Archdiocese of New York*

Birth of Elizabeth

ELIZABETH Ann Bayley was born in New York to Dr. Richard Bayley and his wife Catherine Charlton on August 28, 1774. She was baptized in the Protestant Episcopal Church.

Elizabeth remained a member of this Church until she reached the age of 30.

With the American Declaration of Independence on July 4, 1776, she became one of the first American citizens.

Elizabeth was only three years old when her mother died. One year later her little sister Kitty also died.

Elizabeth's Faith in God

ONE day Elizabeth and her little friend were looking out of a window. Turning toward the sky, Elizabeth said:

"Look, Emma, God lives there, in heaven. All good children will go to Him. Mommy and Kitty went to heaven. They are with God."

Elizabeth's Love for Her Father

ELIZABETH'S father was a Health Inspector of the Port of New York and a Professor of Anatomy at Columbia University.

Elizabeth lived alone with her father, whom she loved dearly. But she did not see him very much.

He was a doctor and he had to be in dangerous places on the war front.

The American colonies were trying to obtain their freedom from England and they needed the help of all their citizens.

Dr. Bayley did all he could to help his fellow Americans while the war continued. It lasted for seven years, but when it was over America was an independent country.

Elizabeth Imitates
Her Father's Kindness

ELIZABETH'S father was often called to help poor families when someone was sick.

He taught his little daughter to be kind to those who needed help.

Elizabeth's Love
for All God's Creatures

WHILE playing with some of her cousins at her uncle's home in New Rochelle, Elizabeth found a bird's nest.

Her cousins picked the little eggs and some of the chicks fell to the ground. Elizabeth took them into her hands. She cried and told her cousins not to touch the eggs.

She put the chicks on some leaves so that the mother could feed them.

When Elizabeth was four years old, her father married Charlotte Amelia Barclay. They later had seven children who were Elizabeth's step-brothers and sisters.

Elizabeth's Love for Her Brothers

ELIZABETH was happy to have so many brothers and sisters to play with. She loved each of them.

Elizabeth Marries William Seton

ELIZABETH grew up to be a fine young woman. She was very beautiful and bright.

All who met her liked her and she made many friends.

Among her good friends was William Magee Seton who had just arrived from Europe where he was studying.

He fell in love with Elizabeth and married her in 1794. He was 26 years old, and she was 19.

A Happy Family

ELIZABETH and William wanted to have a family. They wanted to bring children into the world and make them children of God by Baptism.

In 1795, their first child was born and baptized as Anna Maria. Then four other children followed: William, Richard, Catherine, and Rebecca.

Elizabeth and William were kept busy in bringing up these active children. But they were very happy.

The Family Meets with Misfortune

WILLIAM was a handsome, wealthy businessman. He worked with his father who owned many ships.

When the French Revolution broke out in 1793, many American ships were seized or destroyed. His money in England was taken by the government.

After his father died, William was left with the business and the care of twelve brothers, besides his wife and his own children. The business failed.

Elizabeth Loses Her Husband

WILLIAM'S health was very poor. Doctors told him to take a trip to Italy, where the weather was mild. Elizabeth and her husband had to sell what they owned to pay for the trip.

They also had to leave behind four of their little children. Only Anna Maria, the oldest who was now eight years old, would go with them.

On October 2, 1803, they sailed for Livorno (Leghorn), Italy. After a month in the hospital of the Italian port, Elizabeth's husband died of tuberculosis.

The Filicchi brothers, Anthony and Philip, were friends of William during his student days. They welcomed the widow and the little child to their home and treated them as members of their own family.

Elizabeth Visits a Catholic Church

ELIZABETH wrote to her sister-in-law: "The Filicchi family is very kind to us. Truly, since we left our country, we have met with kindness and thoughtfulness.

"Anna Maria tells me: 'Mommy, how many good friends has God given us in this foreign land.' Their love means so much to me."

The Filicchi family took Elizabeth and her little daughter on a trip to Florence. For the first time in her life Elizabeth went to a Catholic church.

She wrote in a letter: "When I entered the church, I fell to my knees. I cried when I thought for how long I had been away from the house of the Lord.

"I prayed there a long time because I felt that God was really present there."

Elizabeth Learns about the Catholic Religion

ELIZABETH returned to Livorno with her friends. She saw the Catholic faith in action in the good example of her family friends.

They gave her books to study and they prayed for her.

Elizabeth Prays for the Catholic Faith

ELIZABETH herself prayed earnestly that God would give her the light to walk in the way that leads to Him.

She prayed: "O my God and Father. Your word is truth. I beg You to give me faith, hope, and love. This is what I need and what I want."

Elizabeth wrote to her sister-in-law: "My dear sister! How happy we would be if we could believe as these good people do.

"They have the faith in God in the Blessed Sacrament. They find Him in their churches. They see Him coming to them when they are sick.

"I cannot believe that there are any worries in this world if you believe the way Catholics believe."

Return to New York

IT was time to return to New York. Because of the danger on the trip, Mr. Filicchi accompanied them. They were very happy.

Anna Maria asked: "Mommy, are we going to go to a church like we did here when we are back in our own country?"

Elizabeth's Sadness on Leaving Her Friends

AND yet Elizabeth was sad to leave behind such good friends. She wrote:

"The closer a soul is to God, the more it grows in love for all creatures made by Him, and especially for those with whom we are so much in love."

Elizabeth Is Reunited with Her Children

AFTER a voyage of fifty-six days, the ship arrived in New York on June 4. Elizabeth's four children were waiting for them at the pier, together with other members of her family.

Elizabeth wrote: "I have always had young children at home, loving them, waiting to help them, and make them happy.

"I pray that I may live long to be useful to my children. Whatever is the will of the Almighty, I hope I can do His will."

Elizabeth Becomes a Catholic

ELIZABETH was willing to make any sacrifice to do God's will. Five months of study with the kind and devout Filicchis had convinced Elizabeth of the truth of the Catholic Faith.

But the gift of faith and obedience to it came only after a long struggle. She was received into the Catholic Church in New York on March 14, 1805.

She cried out with joy: "Finally God is mine and I am His!"

Elizabeth wrote that the three things that led her to become a Catholic were: belief in the Real Presence of Jesus in the Blessed Sacrament, devotion to Mary the Mother of God, and conviction that the Catholic Church led back to the Apostles and to Christ.

Elizabeth Starts a School

MANY of her family and friends rejected Elizabeth because she became a Catholic. To support her children, she opened a school in Baltimore on the advice of Father Du Bourg, Rector of the Seminary of St. Mary at Baltimore.

God blessed her work. Soon the house was too small for the number of girls wishing to attend.

She was joined by other young women who wished to devote themselves to a holy life.

All the children loved Elizabeth

Elizabeth Becomes a Sister

IN 1809 Elizabeth took Religious vows, and as a Sister was allowed to raise her children. Several other women joined her, two of whom were sisters-in-law. They formed a Religious community.

In the summer they moved to Emmitsburg, Maryland, where they opened a private academy for the girls and a free school.

They were called the Sisters of Charity of St. Joseph. They followed the Rule of St. Vincent de Paul.

Doing the Will of God

ELIZABETH told her Sisters: "In our daily work we must do the will of God; do it in the way He wills it, and because He wills it."

Both the community and the school grew, even though the trials for Mother Seton were heavy.

Some of the Sisters died of tuberculosis. Her two daughters Anna Maria and Rebecca also died of the disease. Living conditions were poor. She accepted all with courage and hope.

Elizabeth's Trust in God

ONCE Mother Seton was asked about the greatest grace God had ever given her. She said: "The greatest grace was my having been led to the Catholic Church."

She also said: "Every morning at Mass I offer my work to God, whose blessed will can make me holy and make my work successful. I put myself in God's hands and tell my companions to do the same."

One of her prayers was as follows:

"I bow to You, my God,
in cheerful hope,
that confiding in Your infinite mercy,
assisted by Your powerful grace,
I shall soon arrive at that hour
of unspeakable joy.

But if it is Your will that the spirit
shall yet contend with its dust,
assist me so to conduct myself
through this life
as not to render it an enemy
but a conductor to that happy state."

Elizabeth's Trust in Jesus

ELIZABETH added:

"O my dearest Mother Mary!
How tight I hold her little picture
to show that I trust in her prayers.
How tenderly she loves our souls
bought by the Blood of her Son.

"I kneel before the crucifix
in silent prayer to Jesus.
He is our only hope."

Two Great Devotions

MOTHER Seton began the first American parochial school at Emmitsburg, an infirmary, an orphanage and school at Philadelphia, and an orphanage in New York City.

Mother Seton had two great devotions: doing the will of God and loving Jesus in the Blessed Sacrament and His Blessed Mother.

She said: "I never feel the presence of the Lord so much as when I have been ill. It is as if I were seeing the good Jesus and His holy Mother at my side to cheer me in all the hours of suffering."

She wrote: "God has given me a great deal to do, and I have always preferred, and hope always to prefer, His will to every wish of my own."

Elizabeth's Writings

IN the midst of her busy life, Elizabeth found time to write many letters, a Diary, and several other works, including translations of French books.

Elizabeth Becomes Ill

ONE day Elizabeth became ill. One of her pupils came to see her. Mother Seton said: "God bless you, my dear child. Remember my last lesson: Seek God in all things. Always ask yourself, 'Will God be pleased with what I am going to do?'

"If you do this, God will be with you, and will help you to keep the grace of your First Communion. You will never see me on earth again. We shall meet in heaven. Remember me in your prayers. God bless you."

Death and Sainthood

THE Sisters and all the children were very sad when they heard that Mother Seton was dying. Mother Seton said to her Sisters as they gathered at her bedside: "I am grateful, my Sisters, that you have come to me at this moment. Be children of the Church, looking to heaven! Be thankful to God!

"Soul of Christ, make me holy; Blood of Christ, wash me."

On January 4, 1821, at two o'clock in the morning, Elizabeth Ann Seton died at the age of 46. She was beatified by Pope John XXIII on March 17, 1963, the first American born citizen to become a saint. She was declared a saint by Pope Paul VI on September 14, 1975, and her feastday is January 4.

■■■■■■■■■■■■■■

Six North American religious orders trace their heritage to Mother Seton, the Sisters of Charity of St. Joseph in Maryland, the Sisters of Charity of St. Vincent de Paul of New York, the Sisters of Charity of Cincinnati, the Sisters of Charity of St. Vincent de Paul of Halifax, Nova Scotia, the Sisters of Charity of St. Elizabeth in New Jersey, and the Sisters of Charity of Seton Hill in Pennsylvania. Over 7500 Sisters in all. **31**

Prayer in Honor of St. Elizabeth Ann

L ORD God, You blessed Elizabeth Ann Seton with gifts of grace as wife and mother, educator and foundress, so that she might spend her life in service to Your people.

Through her example and prayers may we learn to express our love for You in love for our fellow men and women. We ask this through Christ our Lord. Amen.